THE VIKINGS ARE COMING!

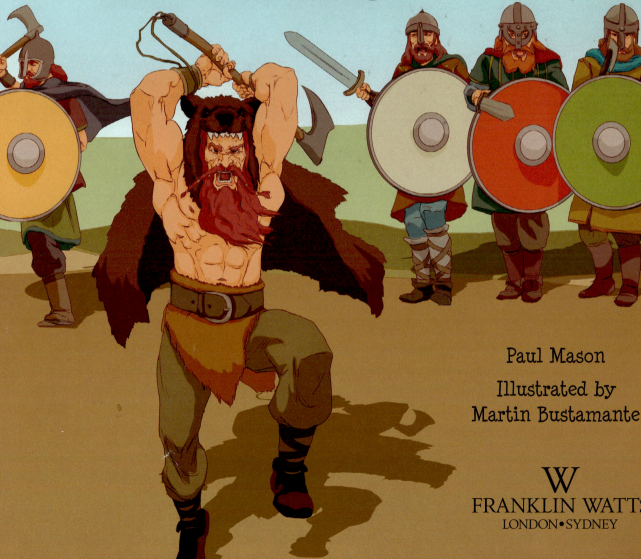

Paul Mason

Illustrated by
Martin Bustamante

W

FRANKLIN WATTS
LONDON • SYDNEY

Franklin Watts
First published in Great Britain in 2018 by
The Watts Publishing Group

Credits
Series Editor: Julia Bird
Illustrator: Martin Bustamante
Packaged by: Collaborate Agency

ISBN 978 1 4451 5692 7

Image Credits

Franklin Watts
An imprint of
Hachette Children's Group
Part of The Watts Publishing Group
Carmelite House
50 Victoria Embankment
London EC4Y 0DZ

An Hachette UK Company
www.hachette.co.uk
www.franklinwatts.co.uk

Printed in China

CONTENTS

Words in **bold** are in the glossary on page 30.

THE VIKING AGE

The name 'Viking' probably comes from an **Old English** word: *wicing*. It meant 'pirate **raider**'. Vikings were possibly the most fearsome raiders ever known.

The Viking homeland

The Vikings came from Scandinavia in northern Europe. Their home countries are known today as Denmark, Norway and Sweden. The Vikings were not a single people. They were made up of groups led by a ruler called a *jarl*. Sometimes, though, groups of Vikings combined to form large forces.

Explorers

The Vikings were skilled sailors and good at **navigation**, and over time they began to journey further and further from their homelands. Viking ships called *knarr* carried goods throughout the known world. They took goods such as amber, furs and wool to trade abroad and received glass, spices, silk and wine in return. There is **archaeological** evidence of Vikings as far west as North America, and as far east as Baghdad (in modern-day Iraq) and Russia.

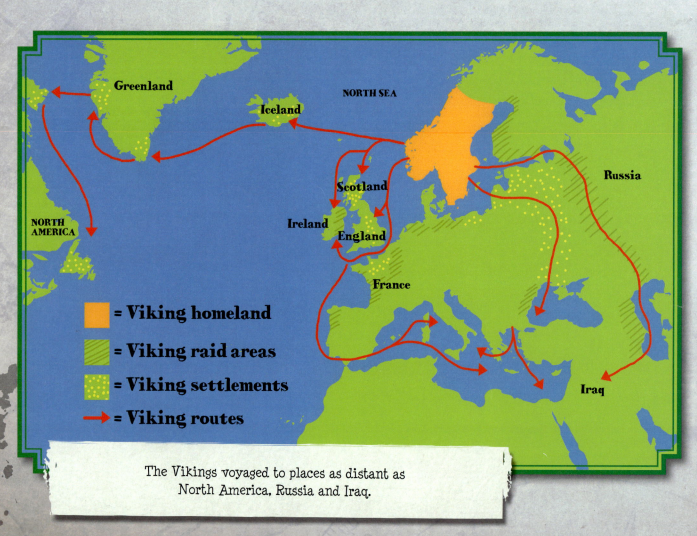

Greenland

NORTH SEA

Iceland

Russia

NORTH AMERICA

Scotland

Ireland

England

France

Iraq

= Viking homeland

= Viking raid areas

= Viking settlements

→ = Viking routes

The Vikings voyaged to places as distant as North America, Russia and Iraq.

Raiders – and invaders

The Viking Age began some time after CE 700 when war parties left Scandinavia to raid nearby lands. They were particularly interested in the wealthy **monasteries** of the British Isles.

The Vikings were also looking for new land to build farms and settlements. But these lands usually already belonged to someone else. To win them, raiding was not enough. The Vikings had to invade. Why the Vikings wanted new lands is not certain. It may have been because their cold, mountainous homelands were not good for farming, or had become too crowded.

In CE 865, a great Viking army invaded England. At this time England was divided into different kingdoms, each ruled by its own leader (see page 27). The Vikings gained control of the Anglo-Saxon kingdoms one after another. By CE 878, only Wessex was left unconquered.

The people of Wessex knew one thing for sure – the Vikings were coming for them next.

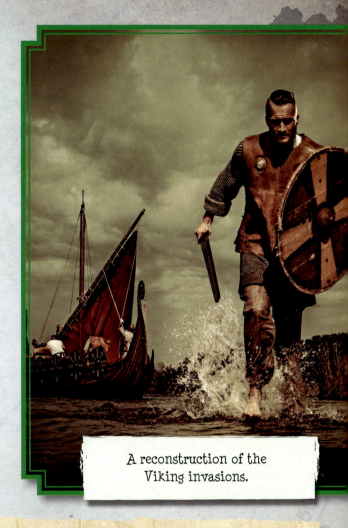

A reconstruction of the Viking invasions.

HOW DO WE KNOW?

How do we know what the Vikings were like? The evidence comes from a variety of **sources**.

The Vikings left behind archaeological evidence. Their weapons, settlements, jewellery and cooking equipment, for example, all tell us about the Viking world.

People who fought the Vikings also left written records that tell us about them. Of course, the Vikings – whom they usually called 'Danes' – were enemies, so we have to be careful about what they say.

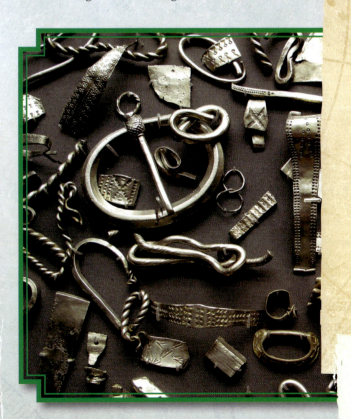

A few of the thousands of pieces of silver and gold Viking jewellery found on the banks of the River Ribble in northern England.

THE VIKINGS ARE COMING!

That was a tough crossing to England! We Vikings are great sailors, as everyone knows – but four days is still a long time to spend in an **open boat** on cold, rough seas.

ACROSS THE SEA

Of course, Vikings have been crossing the North Sea to England for years. Every man on our longship has been here before. We have all felt the fear and excitement of raiding a village or a Christian monastery. The local rulers and kings have never been able to do much about our raids. This time, though, we are not here to raid, but to invade.

THE STORY SO FAR

This invasion began a lifetime ago. A Viking army landed in the kingdom of East Anglia in 865, led by the three sons of the great jarl Ragnar Lodbrok. The East Anglian king, Edmund, was forced to allow the army to spend the winter there. Then the Vikings moved north, into the kingdom of Northumbria. They captured Eboracum, one of the great Anglo-Saxon towns, and renamed it Jorvik. More and more of England fell under Viking control. Now only Wessex resists.

WEALTH AND POWER

When the invasion of England is finally complete, many of us will become rich in silver and land. Ever since it began, men have been coming from across the Viking world to join the invasion force. Not all of them arrived from Scandinavia. Vikings have also travelled here after **reaving** in France and Ireland.

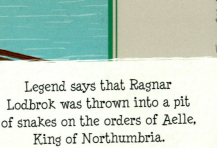

Legend says that Ragnar Lodbrok was thrown into a pit of snakes on the orders of Aelle, King of Northumbria.

HOW DO WE KNOW?

The story of the Viking invasion is told in a book called the *Anglo-Saxon Chronicle*. It says that the invasion was started by the sons of Ragnar Lodbrok, as revenge for his killing by the Northumbrian king, Aelle.

The *Anglo-Saxon Chronicle* had many authors, and it was constantly revised and added to. It was also written by Anglo-Saxons, who were the Vikings' enemies. It is a useful source, but most experts agree that it is not completely reliable.

LONGSHIPS

We Vikings build all kinds of ships – little fishing vessels, rowing boats and transport ships called knarrs. But our most famous ships, the ones that strike fear into our enemies, are our longships.

STEALTH RAIDS

Without longships, we could not have become such feared raiders. They are narrow and long and they float in shallow water. This makes them perfect for travelling quietly up rivers, looking for places to launch a surprise attack. On a sea coast, a longship can be landed on a beach, then pushed off again after the raid for a fast getaway. The smallest type of longship, the *snekkja*, can even be carried short distances by its crew.

People are often surprised when they see a longship at how far we can travel in them. It's true, there's not much shelter aboard! But Viking longships have travelled thousands of *sjømil*. Longships have visited Iceland, Greenland and even North America.

Carved dragons on the front are why people also call them 'dragon ships'.

This *snekkja* is a small longship, with about ten oars on each side.

FINDING THE WAY

Vikings have all sorts of tricks up our sleeves for finding the right route at sea. Old rhymes and chants tell us the way along coasts. Out on the wide ocean we use the stars in the night sky and the gathering-places of sea creatures as a guide to where we are. Birds help us work out how far we are from land, and which land it is.

The ship's **keel** is a long single piece of wood. It makes the boat stronger and stiffer.

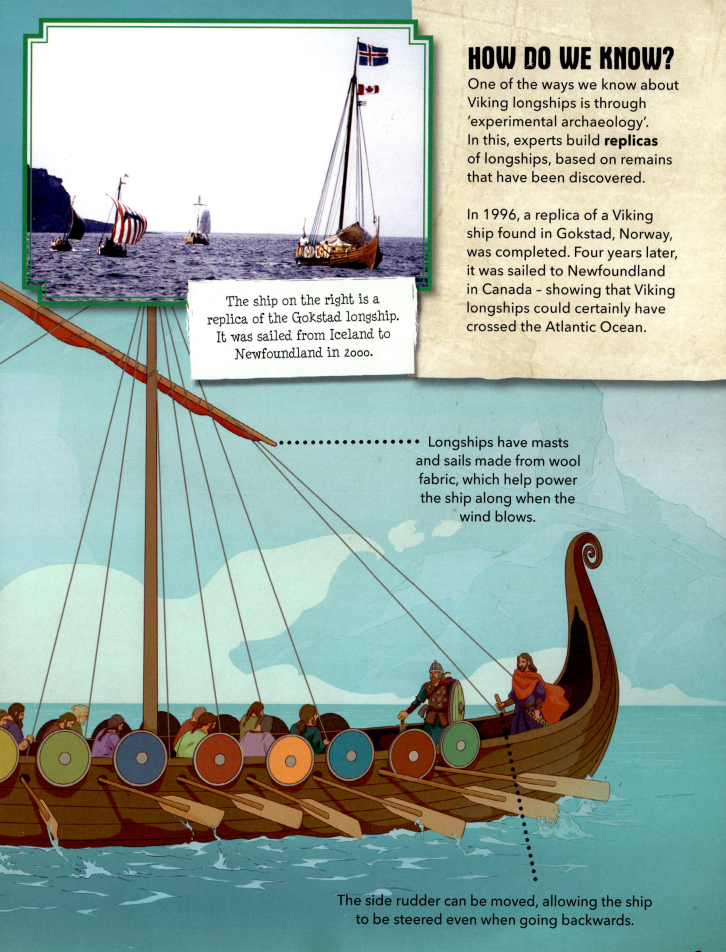

HOW DO WE KNOW?

One of the ways we know about Viking longships is through 'experimental archaeology'. In this, experts build **replicas** of longships, based on remains that have been discovered.

In 1996, a replica of a Viking ship found in Gokstad, Norway, was completed. Four years later, it was sailed to Newfoundland in Canada – showing that Viking longships could certainly have crossed the Atlantic Ocean.

The ship on the right is a replica of the Gokstad longship. It was sailed from Iceland to Newfoundland in 2000.

Longships have masts and sails made from wool fabric, which help power the ship along when the wind blows.

The side rudder can be moved, allowing the ship to be steered even when going backwards.

VIKING WARRIORS

Of course, Alfred of Wessex is wise enough to be scared of our warriors. After all, since the invasion began we have conquered every major English kingdom but his.

Helmet of leather or iron

Viking warriors are well-armed, experienced, fearless fighters. Even before the invasion they had already carved out bases in Scotland, England and Ireland.

The best swords are handed down through families, and have names like 'death giver'.

Axes are favourite Viking weapons.

Chainmail is worn by only the most important, wealthy Vikings. Most wear tough leather armour.

Warriors carry a wooden shield, painted with the warrior's own design.

An under-shirt and trousers are made of wool.

Leather shoes

THE VIKING SHIELD WALL

When Vikings fight as a group we often form a *skjaldborg* – a shield wall. At the front are the young warriors, hungry for glory. They link shields, forming a barrier to enemy attacks. Behind this are the older, more experienced fighters. The battle starts with throwing spears and shooting arrows at the enemy. If this does not decide things, the actual fighting begins.

These modern-day Vikings are ready for 'battle' at a mock fight in Calgary, Canada.

CLASH OF THE SHIELDS

Of course, the Anglo-Saxons also know how to make a shield wall. When two shield walls clash, the result is a massive shoving match between people armed with pointy weapons. The side with the most men, and the best weapons and armour, usually wins.

Sometimes we use a tactic called *svinfylking*. The warriors move into a pointed formation. It drives forward into the enemy, piercing their shield wall and forcing them apart.

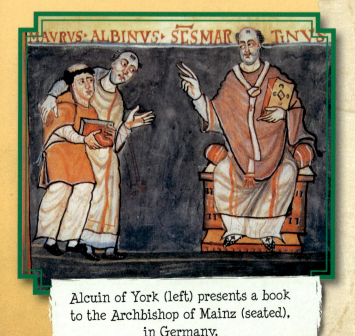

Alcuin of York (left) presents a book to the Archbishop of Mainz (seated), in Germany.

HOW DO WE KNOW?

One of the ways we know about Viking raiders is from letters written by Alcuin of York. Alcuin was an important Anglo-Saxon priest. After the monastery of St Cuthbert was raided by Vikings, Alcuin wrote to the bishop:

'The **pagans** have **desecrated** God's sanctuary, shed the blood of saints around the altar, laid waste the house of our hope and trampled the bodies of the saints like **dung** in the street.'

Alcuin had some advice for those who had survived: 'Stand like men, fight bravely and defend the camp of God.'

BERSERKERS!

There is one thing more terrifying to the Anglo-Saxons than a heavily armed Viking army. It's a heavily armed Viking army, accompanied by a berserker.

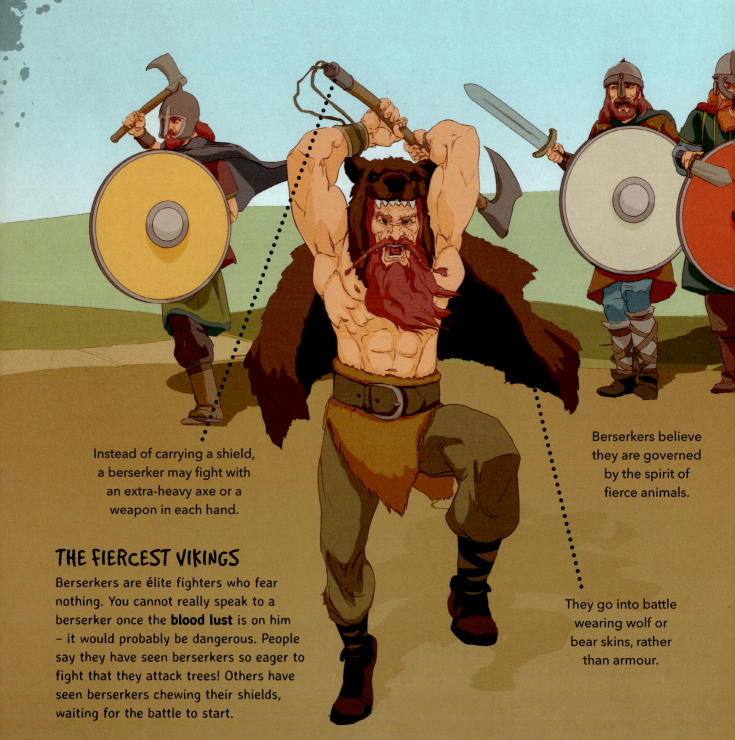

Instead of carrying a shield, a berserker may fight with an extra-heavy axe or a weapon in each hand.

Berserkers believe they are governed by the spirit of fierce animals.

They go into battle wearing wolf or bear skins, rather than armour.

THE FIERCEST VIKINGS

Berserkers are élite fighters who fear nothing. You cannot really speak to a berserker once the **blood lust** is on him – it would probably be dangerous. People say they have seen berserkers so eager to fight that they attack trees! Others have seen berserkers chewing their shields, waiting for the battle to start.

ODIN'S PROTECTION

The berserkers believe they fight with the protection of the god Odin. Odin is a war god and gives them special powers. This is why berserkers feel they cannot be defeated and do not need to wear any kind of protection in battle.

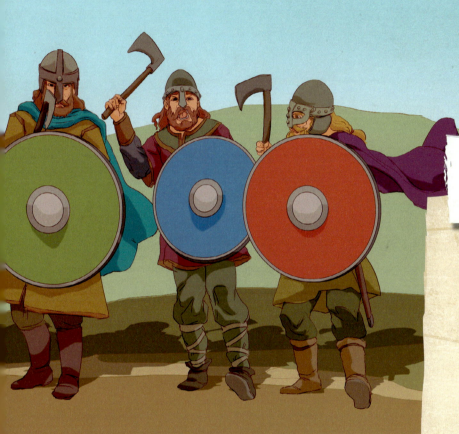

This carving from the 6th century shows two berserkers. The warrior on the right wears a wolf's-head mask.

BERSERKERS IN ACTION

Once the fighting does begin, berserkers show no fear. They charge forward, howling like wolves or growling like bears. They do not seem to feel pain – even if they are wounded, berserkers do not retreat or stop fighting. In fact, they are so fierce that they can be hard to control. Battles are sometimes lost because the berserkers at the front charge into the enemy and leave a hole in their own side's shield wall!

HOW DO WE KNOW?

Berserkers are first mentioned in an **epic** called *Haraldskvadet*, which was written some time in the 800s. They are also mentioned in *Grettir's Saga*, the story of an Icelandic outlaw:

'They had wolf-coverings as mail ... and iron didn't bite them; one of them ... started roaring and bit the edge of his shield ... and growled viciously.'

Another source, the *Volsunga Saga*, says the berserkers:

'... went without armour, were as mad as dogs and wolves, they bit their shields, were as strong as bears or oxen, they killed everybody, and neither fire nor iron bit them; this is called going berserk.'

THE WAR ON WESSEX

Wessex is the only Anglo-Saxon kingdom we have not invaded and conquered. Its riches are what drew many of us here – and now, at last, they are within reach.

GUTHRUM'S ARMY

Our army has gathered around Guthrum, the greatest Viking warlord in England. Five years ago, the Anglo-Saxons paid us silver and gold to leave Wessex, when we might have conquered it. Guthrum has decided they have been left in peace for long enough!

ATTACKING WESSEX

After we joined Guthrum's force, we slipped past the Wessex defences and met up with another Viking army coming from the west. Together we captured the town of Wareham, on the coast near Alfred's biggest town, Winchester. But Alfred gathered an army far bigger than ours to re-take Wareham. We were surrounded, outnumbered and getting ready to die ... when Alfred let us leave if we promised not to come back! We promised – and he let us go.

VIKING GAINS

They say Alfred is the cleverest man in England, but it seems doubtful. The next year, 877, we were back, raiding Wessex again. More and more territory was captured, including the town of Exeter. Here, Alfred and Guthrum made yet another peace deal. The men say Alfred paid us to leave.

Whatever happened, the result was that we spent early winter in the kingdom of Mercia – right next door to Wessex. Something tells me that we might be back there soon.

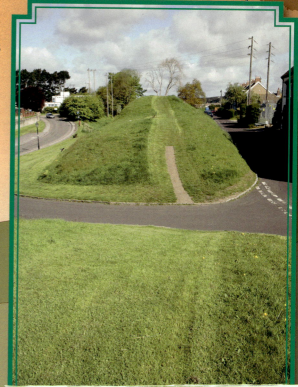

This stretch of an Anglo-Saxon earthwork in Wareham is known as Bloody Bank.

HOW DO WE KNOW?

Alfred learned his lesson from the Viking occupation of Wareham. He had the town fortified, to make it harder to capture. In fact, Alfred set up a whole series of fortified towns around his kingdom.

Today, the remains of these fortifications can still be seen in many places, including Wareham. Archaeologists sometimes find old Viking and Anglo-Saxon weapons at places where the towns were attacked.

VIKING SETTLERS

At first, every Viking who came to England was a raider. Next came the invaders. Once we controlled some lands, Viking settlers began to arrive. They were not fighters but craftsmen, traders, women and children.

FARMING FOLK

Most Vikings are not fearsome warriors. Many Vikings are actually farmers, just like the Anglo-Saxons. Maybe this isn't so surprising. After all, the places we come from are not so different from the places they came from, hundreds of years ago.

VIKING LIFE

Everyday life on a Viking farm isn't much different from life on an Anglo-Saxon one. People wear similar wool clothes, and mostly eat similar food. They have bread, cheese and eggs, and eat meat from chickens, sheep, pigs or animals they have hunted. Fish and wild fruit are popular. People drink mainly water, or perhaps milk.

LONGHOUSES

Vikings often live together in a big building called a longhouse. These are shaped like a long box and have thatched or turf roofs. The floor of a longhouse is often dug below ground level, which helps keep out draughts. In cold weather, people share with their animals. It gets pretty smoky and smelly!

HOW DO WE KNOW?

Archaeology from Viking settlements tells us what their houses were like. The remains of many longhouses have been discovered, including this famous one at Mosfellsbær, near Reykjavik in Iceland. It is thought to date back to the 11th century.

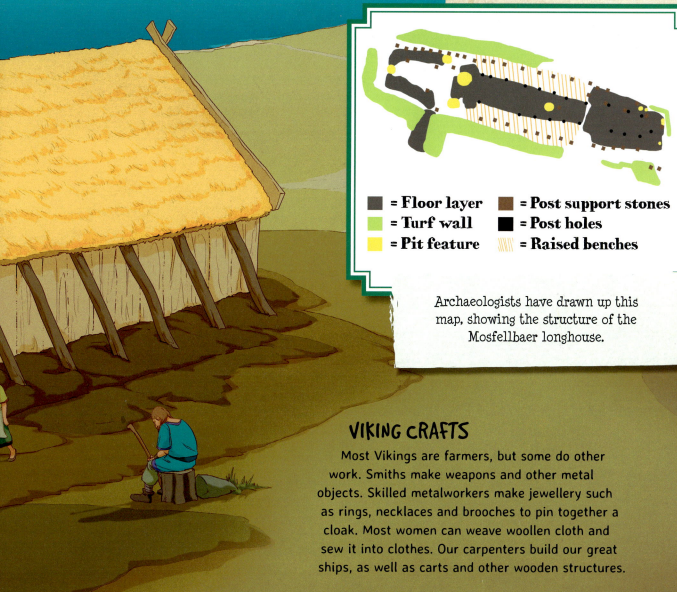

■ = Floor layer   ■ = Post support stones
■ = Turf wall   ■ = Post holes
■ = Pit feature   ▨ = Raised benches

Archaeologists have drawn up this map, showing the structure of the Mosfellbaer longhouse.

VIKING CRAFTS

Most Vikings are farmers, but some do other work. Smiths make weapons and other metal objects. Skilled metalworkers make jewellery such as rings, necklaces and brooches to pin together a cloak. Most women can weave woollen cloth and sew it into clothes. Our carpenters build our great ships, as well as carts and other wooden structures.

THE VIKING WAY

Soon, we will be back in Wessex to finish off Alfred and his army. The people there are going to have to get used to living the Viking way.

VIKING LAW

Vikings have never bothered to write down our laws. Instead, we remember them – which does sometimes lead to arguments! When disagreements happen over things like who owns some property, whether one person has injured another or even if a murder has taken place, we sometimes hold a *Thing*. This is a meeting to decide who is right. Everyone has a say, and we vote together on what the outcome should be.

Our punishments include being made an 'outlaw'. Outlaws have to live away from other people. Anyone can hunt them down and kill them.

Sometimes we use a *holmgang* to settle disputes. It's a fight in which the winner is considered to have been favoured by the gods and therefore in the right.

LEADERS AND SLAVES

Viking society is made up of jarls, *karls* and *thralls*. Jarls are the leaders. Many are rich in land, ships and followers. Their followers expect to be rewarded with shares of conquered land and riches. Lately some jarls have become so powerful that they are calling themselves kings.

Ordinary Vikings are karls. We are free people, and can own land and property. Most karls are farmers, though they also know how to fight. Some have skills like shoemaking or metalwork.

The lowest rank among the Vikings is thrall, a **slave**, usually a captured enemy. Thralls do the hardest jobs. When they can no longer work, they are often killed.

Legendary warrior Egill Skallagrímsson prepares to fight a holmgang to settle his argument with another Viking.

HOW DO WE KNOW?

A Viking epic called *Egill's Saga* tells the story of Egill Skallagrímsson. After an argument about wealth, Egill challenges another man to a holmgang and wins.

Several other Viking epics mention holmgang. In some, berserkers used it as a way to get another man's property. This may be why some Viking rulers eventually made holmgang illegal.

FESTIVALS, FOOD AND FEASTS

Vikings love festivals. Even the few Vikings who have become Christians still celebrate our festivals. Christian Anglo-Saxons have actually started adopting our festivals as their own!

THE MIDWINTER FESTIVAL

Where we come from, winters are long and cold. After the shortest day of the year – midwinter – spring and summer are on their way. We celebrate our biggest festival: Jól. We make **offerings** to the gods to celebrate the defeat of winter, then have a huge feast.

The storytellers say that on the night of Jól, the god Odin rides through the sky on his eight-legged horse, Sleipnir. Children leave out their shoes, filled with hay and sugar, to help Sleipnir on his journey. In return for their kindness, Odin leaves them a gift.

OTHER FESTIVALS AND FEASTS

Most of our other big festivals are linked to the seasons: spring, midsummer and harvest. At any festival there should always be a feast, with plenty of meat! A whole animal is usually killed and roasted.

Back home a horse would be **sacrificed**: part would be offered to the gods and the rest would be eaten. Here in England, the Christians complain about sacrifices so most people just eat lamb. To drink, there is beer and **mead**.

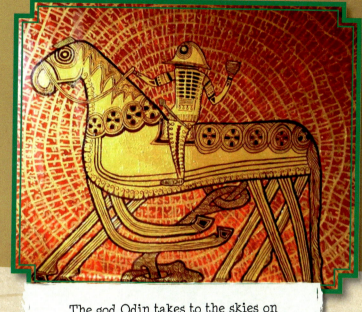

The god Odin takes to the skies on Sleipnir, his eight-legged horse.

HOW DO WE KNOW?

We know about Viking festivals partly because some are still celebrated today. In Sweden, for example, the midsummer festival is an important celebration.

One festival that uses an old Viking name (though it is not a Viking festival) is Christmas. We sometimes call it 'Yule' – which comes from the old Viking name, Jól.

Christmas borrowed other features from the Vikings, too. Santa Claus and his reindeer are based on Odin and Sleipnir. Instead of shoes filled with hay and sugar, people leave out mince pies for Santa on Christmas Eve. Finally, children are given gifts just as they were in Viking times.

GODS AND WARRIORS

The Anglo-Saxons are Christians, but most Vikings are not. We follow our own gods. These are the strong gods that will help us in the battle for Wessex!

MEN AND GODS

Our stories tell us that the world of men is called Midgard. It is one of the worlds found in the branches of the Great Tree, Yggdrasil. There are eight other worlds in Yggdrasil's roots and branches. In some live creatures such as giants, dwarves and elves. Others are home to gods.

Yggdrasil

Asgard

Bifrost

Alfheim

Muspellheim

Midgard

Vanaheim

Nidavellir

Jotunheim

Niflheim

Helheim

VALHALLA, HALL OF THE HEROES

One of Yggdrasil's worlds is called Asgard. Here, Odin has a hall named Valhalla. This is where heroes and warriors go after death. No Viking wants to die in the invasion of Wessex! But if he does die bravely on the battlefield, sword in hand, he will be carried to Valhalla by the Valkyries, Odin's servants. In Valhalla he will feast every night on a magical boar called Sæhrímnir. (This is why at Jól, we always eat pork.)

GODS OF WAR

In the battle for Wessex, many Vikings will be asking for help from two gods in particular: Odin and Thor. Odin is chief of the gods in Asgard. He is wise and cunning – but he also plays tricks, and he is only really interested in powerful war chiefs and berserkers.

For the ordinary Viking, Thor is a much safer god. He is brave and strong. Armed with his mighty war hammer, Mjölnir, Thor is the mightiest warrior in all of the nine worlds.

On the left, Thor wields his war hammer, Mjölnir. Many Viking amulets, like the one above, have been uncovered by archaeologists over the years.

HOW DO WE KNOW?

Over the years, archaeologists have found many **amulets** made of a T-shaped piece of metal and most assumed that they represented Thor's hammer, but they couldn't be sure. However, in 2014, an archaeologist discovered an amulet that had 'THIS IS A HAMMER' carved into it, proving that these amulets really did represent Thor's war hammer. Warriors probably carried them hoping for Thor's protection in battle.

THE BATTLE FOR WESSEX

At the beginning of this year, 878, we launched another attack on King Alfred. This time, our warlord Guthrum was determined to invade Wessex and make it Viking for good.

THE RAID ON CHIPPENHAM

Guthrum knew that Alfred was in Chippenham, just a few hours' ride from our army's winter **quarters.** We raided the town, striking fast to catch Alfred unawares – but he escaped with a few men. Quickly, our main forces crossed into Wessex and spread out into the northern part of the kingdom, hunting for Alfred. If he could be caught, we knew Wessex would be ours.

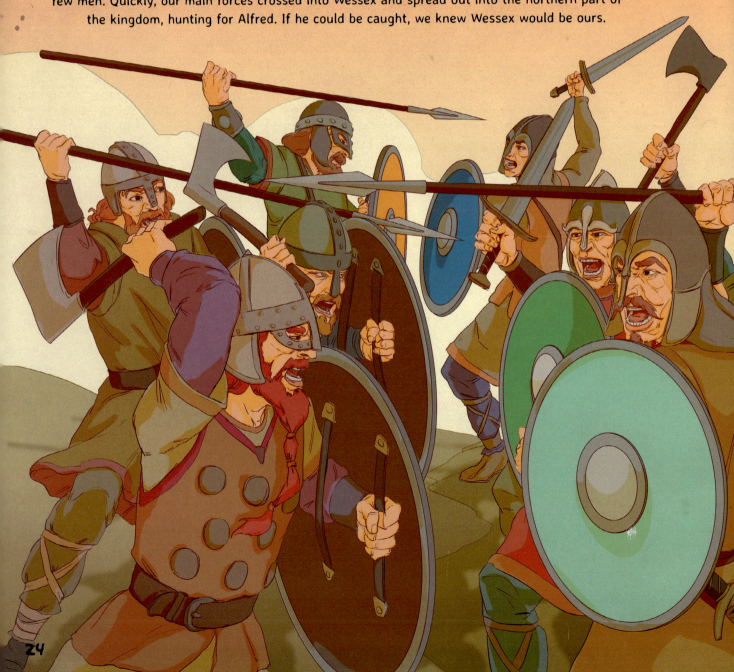

ALFRED GATHERS HIS FORCES

We discovered later that Alfred had hidden on the Isle of Athelney. It's a little island where two rivers meet and is surrounded by treacherous marshes. It's almost impossible to reach unless you know the way. Alfred sent out secret messages to other Anglo-Saxon leaders, telling them his plans to fight back against us.

By spring, Alfred was ready. He called the *fyrd*, the Anglo-Saxon army, to gather at a place called Egbert's Stone. Over two thousand men met him there – a huge force. At last, the battle to decide the future of Wessex was coming.

THE BATTLE OF EDINGTON

The battle finally happened at a place called Edington. The shield walls of the two armies came together and tried to force each other back. Many men died, struck by enemy spears, battle axes, swords or war hammers. The battle lasted all day.

In the end, it was the Viking shield wall that was worn down. There were just so many Anglo-Saxons! However many we killed, new ones just took their place.

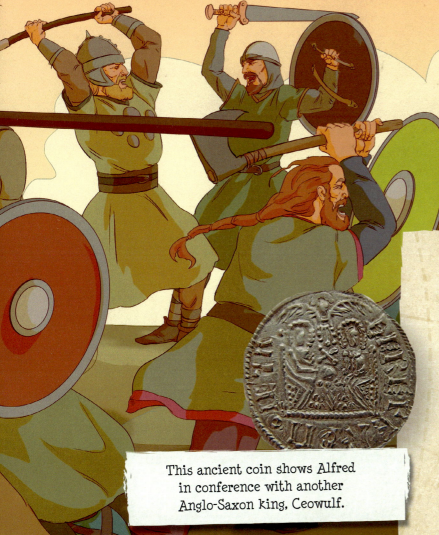

This ancient coin shows Alfred in conference with another Anglo-Saxon king, Ceowulf.

HOW DO WE KNOW?

The *Anglo-Saxon Chronicle* tells us about Alfred's fight against the Vikings. It was written by his supporters and shows Alfred alone saving England. However, this may not be completely true. A coin found in Watlington, Oxford in 2015 shows Alfred side-by-side with another king, Ceowulf II of Mercia. This suggests that Ceowulf was Alfred's ally in the fight.

WESSEX AND THE DANELAW

After the Battle of Edington, our army fled. King Alfred's men chased us back to Chippenham, where our attack on Alfred had begun the invasion of Wessex.

THE SIEGE OF CHIPPENHAM

We took shelter in Alfred's fortress at Chippenham, which was quickly surrounded by Anglo-Saxon warriors. At first there was little to eat inside. Then there was nothing. Soon, we were starving and desperate. After 14 days trapped in the fortress, Guthrum asked to make peace.

THE DANELAW

King Alfred didn't make it easy this time. We had to leave Wessex, of course, and agree to stay in the lands that we already controlled: East Anglia, eastern Mercia and southern Northumbria. This area will be called the Danelaw: Alfred has agreed that it is to be ruled and settled by Vikings. We will not attack Wessex, and Wessex will not attack us.

GUTHRUM BECOMES CHRISTIAN

One thing everyone knows about King Alfred is that he's really keen on Christianity. As part of the peace agreement, Guthrum agreed to become a Christian. He was baptised and given a new, English-sounding name: Aethelstan.

CHANGING TIMES

The warriors are not sure what to think about Guthrum's conversion. Does he mean it, or has he just been forced into it by Alfred? Perhaps Guthrum is right to become Christian. After all, our gods Odin and Thor were on our side in the Battle of Edington – but we still lost. Maybe the Christian god is stronger.

The line between the areas ruled by 'Danes' (Vikings) to the north and Anglo-Saxons to the south.

■ = Anglo-Saxon Kingdoms
■ = The Danelaw
•••• = Watling Street

Northumbria

Jorvik

Mercia

East Anglia

Wales

Wessex

Kent

HOW DO WE KNOW?

After the Anglo-Saxon victory at Edington, Alfred and Guthrum made an agreement. It tells us where the dividing line was drawn between Anglo-Saxon lands and the Danelaw:

*'First concerning our boundaries: up on the Thames, and then up on the Lea, and along the Lea unto its source, then straight to Bedford, then up on the Ouse to **Watling Street**.'*

This line divided England in two, along a line that went from London to the River Mersey.

VIKINGS AND ANGLO-SAXONS

The Anglo-Saxon victory over Guthrum's army in Wessex meant that the Vikings did not take control of the whole of England. But they also did not completely go away.

Losing land

Over the next few years, pieces of the territory ruled by Vikings were recaptured by King Alfred. His son Edward then drove the Viking rulers from power in the whole of southern England. Edward also made the kingdom of Mercia, to the north of Wessex, part of his territory.

Alfred's grandson Athelstan continued the battle against the Vikings. He won a famous victory in northern England against the army of Olaf Guthfrithson at the Battle of Brunanburh. Finally the last Viking leader in England, Eric Bloodaxe, was killed in an ambush in CE 954.

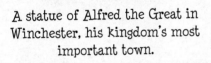
A statue of Alfred the Great in Winchester, his kingdom's most important town.

From invaders to raiders

It was not long before Vikings began raiding the coasts of England again. Now, though, they were not looting treasure from monasteries. Instead they launched large-scale attacks, then waited to be paid to leave. These payments were called *danegeld*. By 991, England was paying 4,500 kg of silver as danegeld. By 1012 it had increased to 22,000 kg.

After their first invasion attempt failed, Vikings carried on raiding the coasts of the British Isles.

The second Viking invasion

In 1013, the Danish king Sweyn Forkbeard invaded England. Three years later, the invasion was complete and Sweyn's son Cnut became king of England. Cnut now married Emma, the widow of England's last Anglo-Saxon king. Anglo-Saxon and Viking people in England were becoming mixed together in a way that was more and more difficult to disentangle.

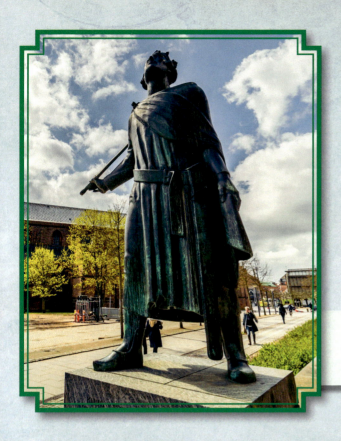

A statue of King Cnut in Denmark, where he was also king.

The Norman invasion

After Cnut, England was ruled by his son Harthacnut, then Emma's son Edward. In 1066, King Edward died without children. Three men wanted be the next ruler of England:

- Harold Godwinson, a powerful noble
- Harald Hardrada of Norway
- William of Normandy, the great-nephew of Emma, Cnut's wife

Harold was crowned King Harold II of England on 6 January 1066. Harald Hardrada invaded, but was defeated by King Harold's army. Harold was then beaten himself at the Battle of Hastings by William – later known as William the Conqueror, King of England. The Norman age had begun.

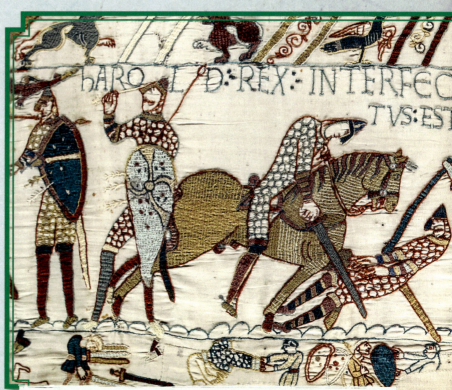

This scene from the Bayeux Tapestry includes the words 'Harold the king is killed'. Historians still debate whether Harold is the man with the arrow in his eye or the one being trampled by a horse.

GLOSSARY

amulet   small piece of jewellery that is worn (usually around the neck) to bring good luck

archaeology   study of actual objects from the past

blood lust   desire to attack and kill something

CE   short for 'Common Era', which refers to a date after the year '0'

desecrate   damage or destroy a holy place

dung   animal waste

epic   long poem, especially one based on traditional stories

keel   the bottom section of a ship

mead   alcoholic drink made using honey, water and spices

monastery   place where men who are members of religious organisations live and work

navigation   the process of planning and following a route to travel somewhere

offering   something precious or valuable that is given to the gods when you want help, or as thanks

Old English   language spoken by Anglo-Saxons until about 1150

open boat   boat without a full deck, which does not have proper shelter

pagan   non-Christian (this is what the word meant to Anglo-Saxons, today it has a different meaning)

quarters   place where a person or group temporarily lives

raider   someone who carries out a sudden, violent attack

reave   carry out raids in order to steal valuables

replica   exact copy of something

sacrifice   to kill an animal or person as part of a ceremony, usually as an offering to the gods

sjømil   Viking measurement of distance; it means 'sea mile', though it measures not a mile but 7.4 km

slave   person whose freedom has been taken away and who is forced to work without payment

source   place something comes from, especially information

Watling Street   ancient road running from south-east to north-west England

Viking names

The Vikings had some great names! Here are some that you (possibly) wish you were called:

The best Viking name ever has to be Eric Bloodaxe, but others include Bjorn Ironside, Ragnar Hairy-Breeks and his son Ivar the Boneless, Sweyn Forkbeard.

Of course, not all Viking names were so impressive: you would not want to be known as Gorm the Old, or Harald Finehair.

Timeline of the Vikings in England

789
Vikings begin their attacks on England.

865
Viking forces launch an invasion of England. They establish a settlement at Jorvik (now called York). By 878, the only big Anglo-Saxon kingdom they have not conquered is Wessex.

878
Anglo-Saxon forces defeat a Viking army at the Battle of Edington. Later, Anglo-Saxon and Viking leaders divide England between them.

FINDING OUT MORE

Places to visit

There are many places you can visit to see objects from the Viking world. Here are just a few:

The **British Museum** owns many objects from the time of the Anglo-Saxons and Vikings, and is a great place to see old Viking helmets, weapons and craftwork. There is more information about the museum on its website www.britishmuseum.org.

The website section on Anglo-Saxons and Vikings for teachers and schoolchildren can be found here: tinyurl.com/cdunho2.

The **Jorvik Viking Centre** in York is a brilliant place to find out about the Vikings: where they came from, how they lived, and the ways they contributed to the development of England. Until 2020 the Jorvik Centre will be displaying some of the British Museum's most famous Viking items. The centre also has an excellent website at jorvikvikingcentre.co.uk.

At the **National Museum of Scotland** there are many Viking objects, including a model of a longship and Viking swords, combs and jewellery. The museum's website is at nms.ac.uk.

The **Ancient Technology Centre** in Dorset is home to a recreation of a Viking longhouse, which it took volunteers and groups of schoolchildren three years to build.

Books to read

Ivar the Boneless and the Vikings David Gill (Franklin Watts, 2016)

The life and times of the most important leader of the Viking attempt to invade Britain: Ivar the Boneless. Ivar was a terrifying enemy, a warlord so fierce he is said never to have lost a battle.

Stars of Mythology: Viking Nancy Dickmann (Franklin Watts, 2017)

Introducing the gods, goddesses, monsters and heroes of Viking myths – in their own words (possibly…).

The Best (And Worst) Jobs in Anglo-Saxon and Viking Times Clive Gifford (Wayland, 2017)

This book is a great introduction to the kinds of jobs people did in Anglo-Saxon and Viking Britain. From an egg collector to a jewellery-maker, this is the place to find out what kind of Viking job you would have wanted to apply for.

991
The Anglo-Saxon king Ethelred pays danegeld to the Vikings after their victory at the Battle of Maldon, in Essex. It is said to have been 3,300 kg of silver.

1000
The Viking Leif Erikson explores the coast of North America.

1013
The Viking king Sweyn Forkbeard launches an invasion of England. The invasion succeeds, and three years later his son Cnut is crowned king.

INDEX